THE BLISS OF A MOMENT

THE BLISS OF A MOMENT

BENOY KUMAR SARKAR

GYAN

Published by

Gyan Publishing House
5, Ansari Road
Daryaganj, New Delhi-110002
Phone: 011-47034999, 9811692060
E-mail: books@gyanbooks.com

Distribution Network
gyanbooks.com
India, USA, Canada, UK, Australia, France

ISBN: 978-81-212-8578-0 (PB)
First Published, 1918

2nd Impression 2023

Printed at: Gyan Press, Delhi.

THE BLISS OF A MOMENT
Author: Benoy Kumar Sarkar

THE BLISS OF A MOMENT

BY

BENOY KUMAR SARKAR

BOSTON
THE POET LORE COMPANY
THE GORHAM PRESS

PREFACE.

All these poems have been written in English from the original Bengali by the author himself. All the pieces in Part IV (except two) are, as indicated in the titles, extracts from longer poems, which are studies in situations and attitudes. A few appeared in the "Conservator."

BENOY KUMAR SARKAR.

April 26, 1918.

CONTENTS

I. The Call of the Sea

II. Flesh and Blood

CONTENTS

III. Sights and Sounds

CONTENTS

CONTENTS

V. PERSONALITY

I

THE CALL OF THE SEA

THE ATLANTIC IN STORM

Here at last is the ocean indeed
Full of boisterous dancing wild;
Only then is a life being lived by man
When stir and turmoil rule his self.

It is laughter this moment and crying next,
Playing and singing then again;
No story of rest, no message of peace
Finds echo in heroic hearts.

Changes on changes' heels I see around me
In the sport of colours and waves;
Here in this full swing of wanton revels
No rules and canons one can find.

Foolish that thou thinkest perchance thou hast
Caught life's being firm within thy hands;
Forthwith insolently thee it eludes
In splashing, booming, breaking gait.

Whenever once thou understandest life,
Its dignity is surely lost;
But that it is not ever to be grasped
Is its grand mystery and strength.

Thou, in love with storm, inviting ruin,
Thy waves bombarding the highest decks,
O Atlantic, my companion long,
Aeons thy spirit in me dwells!

THE BOUNDLESS

Look not to the sea for the infinite,
It is the human life that boundless is;
Who would call that an unlimited being
Whose measurements are to all known and fixed?

The sea's limits were found by sailing boats
Of merchants, Phoenician, Hindu, Greek;
Subdued and ruled are the vast blue waters
Today by electricity and steam.

The weight of every quart of brine you know,
Of the polar as of the tropic seas;
You know where the depth is Himâlayan height,
Also the deeper and shallower beds.

The metric standard has gauged the billows,
The ocean floor has tendered its contents;
How far down the surface pass heat and light
Is perceptible to extended touch and sight.

The Gulf Stream's path and speed are all chalked
out,
Scheduled are the exact times of the tides,
You can write out the correct horoscope
Of the monsoons and the trade winds of the globe.

By man's strength is the universe always
Of an infinite's mystery deprived;
The only adorable on earth, then, is
The limitless life, love, hatred of man.

THE SONGS OF THE SEA

Of what doth the sea sing? Its breath exhales
The story of the whole universe!
Every bubble of its wavy self
Reveals kinship with the sun, moon, and stars.

It kisses the sky's vapour from the air,
Fishes and plants in its womb praise the skies;
Its garments are the gifts from light and clouds,
The blue deeps are thus tinged purple, dark, green;
Minerals and salts does the land help it with,
The sea's returns are but the soils dissolved.

To the sea the rivers bring the spirit
Of thousands of villages and cities;
Of what else can the lord of rivers sing
But of the life that men and women live?

All the forces are concentrated here,
Sweet and terrible, bright and dark, life and death;
From this reservoir of unnumbered gems
A message of unending strength does rise;
The boundless ocean with its trumpet call
Is the perennial energy's bard.

AN AUTUMN NIGHT ON THE PACIFIC

The waves by day got their hues from the sky,
The dark night makes the sky dance to the waves.

Lo, there, the lamp at the top of the mast,—
How frantic it leaps to rival the stars!

Reddish, bright, or faint do the planets gleam,
They travel lonesome, coupled, or in groups.

Up in the dome's ceiling gems countless burn,
Down, the dark carpet is ruffled by the wind.

Darkness has reduced the watery sheet,
Reduced the volume of the ocean's roof;
Too quick are left the new horizons behind,
And fresh clouds on fresh arches greet the eyes.

The stars are rising and setting at will,
The constellations sojourn on their rounds,
But peaceless and full of turbulence heaves
The Pacific's breast in an autumn night.

THE SEA AS MOTION

Art thou motion incarnate, O wild sea?
Is thy restlessness at once thy strength and grace?

In movement the soul of beauty lies;
Hast thou worn that as thy dress on all limbs?
I see thy billows at riotous play
Are but lines geometric on the dance.

Up thy million hands something to grasp,
Watchful inconstant thy myriad eyes,
Full of desires is thy passionate face,
Thy breast surges with bitter griefs and pangs.

Surely of thy treasure art thou deprived,
Parted from beloved, perchance, thou art,
Or what thou seekest eludes ever thy grasp,—
Is this what maddens thee and stirs thy frame?

It is wants that awaken thy spirit,
O thou beauty in destruction's guise!
Whosoever carries a hungry heart
Must embody the soul of revolt.

TSU-SHIMA SEA

The sea of Tsu-shima kisses the foot
Of Korean hills at Fusan,
The mists have covered the thatched huts ashore
And dark clouds enveloped the sky.

The sea looks pitch-black from its cloudy tent,
The ship-cleft waters bubble blue in white,
Liquid silver glimmers at spots not far
Whereon the sun can dart its beams.

Yonder, Tsu-shima, the "isle of pines" evergreen,
Here, the sea under rainy skies,—
Both have witnessed the marvellous battle
By which Japan has saved the East.

To crush Nippon came the Russian fleet,
Its grave it found through Togo's skill;
Asia's Salamis, then, is this,
And Port Arthur, the Marathon, there.

THE MESSAGE OF THE SEA

To the heroic soul the sea appears
As youth full of breakings and makings fresh;
The mind that creates ideals discovers
Ever new forms on the sea's breast emerge.

What is the sea in the scientist's eyes?
Revolt and struggle at every step;
The mystic rapt in meditation reads
Here the message of the Eternal Self.

Beauteous both as sweet and austere,
The sea inspires poets to lofty verse,—
The strain that proceeds therefrom is a spur
To noble freedom, full and simple life.

Love itself is the sea to the lovers' gaze,
Swelling with longings, calm when satisfied;
Joy's self it is to those that are alive,
To the oppressed it is but cries and tears.

The past, present, future, ages, cycles,—
All that limitless is, are the sea's walls;
The stillness of the midnight it evokes
And the deepest gloom of the dark fortnight.

II

FLESH AND BLOOD

THE RAW FLESH

Lo, there, the Santals are issuing forth
In bands with yells for the game or the chase;
They would cross the woods and would jostle the
beasts ,
Thus would their appetites be whetted sharp.

And, here, the fifty youths seven hours long
Are swimming on the breast of the ocean;
Ten miles of water they are making now,
Tomorrow they are sure to break the world.

The hugest trees are being sliced to pieces
By the single woodman's unaided axe;
The vigorous tide of his warm life-blood
No philosopher could ever surmise.

The farmer in his cot a free man is,
A nucleus of energy his home;
The butcher enjoys the verve of raw life,
Not in the attorney's rooms does this flow.

Two meals a day the workman cannot earn,
He dare not bear the burden of a wife;
All the same his life-long heart-scorching sighs
Amass rebellion's clouds in the sky.

New goods they find in waters, hills, and mines,
In forests and soils they discover new wealth,
Their spirits are pure, their blood unalloyed,
They are bound to generate novel worlds.

LIVING

No such thing as religion
Has ever existed on earth;
It is the ways and means of living
That weaklings religion call.

What the mighty enjoy today
Is tomorrow principles named;
Do masters ever follow rules?
Laws guide but apprentice-work.

To save one's life one has recourse
To tiger's leaps or snake's zigzags;
The hero's movements press and crush,
Which child of man not a hero is?

Man that is man is bound to break
And demolish barriers old;
All human blood, no matter whose,
Seeks to challenge the questions closed.

Life I know, it is human heart,
It smells flesh, and is streams of blood ,
No faiths and morals it cares for,
It loves fresh youth's creative urge.

TRUTH IN ART

To diverse melodies they tune their songs,
Could all these strains ever appeal to your ears?
Varied steps you try in your rounds of dance,
Do all these find an echo in my heart?

Jealousy and enmity he has not felt,
The world's ways are thus unknown to his mind;
You have not tasted the mystery of love,
So eyeless you rove about on the earth.

Intoxicated with liquor I live,
Some men are warned to self-control by this;
Others there are who believe that with wine
I have expanded the bounds of my soul.

The miner cares for the stones in mountains,
But you are there in search of drugs or birds;
I seek responses from mimosa plants,
His heart is bound to the engine of steam.

You are enlarging the rights of the poor,
The freedom of slaves engages his mind;
One woman loves the husband as her god,
Another calls wifehood a slavery old.

Destruction's easy way seems in your eyes
What I have created for mankind's good;
You are as great a critic of life as I,
Only you and I agree to differ.

Life's experiences of all of us
Are true to our individual selves;
Art, science, philosophy are thus born
To declare only those personal truths.

THE VOICE OF THE PARIAH

Not in a day have you acquired
Wisdom or wealth and skill or strength,
Not in a life-time have you built up
The family's name or prestige of clan.

Of character, learning and riches
Your forefathers the foundations laid;
You look immense and big no doubt,
But on your ancestors' shoulders,
And like money secure in safety vaults
Virtues are yours by accident of birth!

No past tradition have we, no forbears,
No stories narrating family deeds;
No relatives and kinsfolk are our pride,
No distinguished house does our conduct set;
No sense of shame therefore is born with us,
Nor care we what we omit or commit.

The A, B, C, we are but commencing,
The first steps of a history we would lay,
Our capital is fresh blood and muscles
And the experience of whole mankind.

At the zenith brightly shines your sun,
We are but at the dawn of life's career;
No other difference on earth is there
Between us two, the risen and the rising.

UNREST

Incessant are they in their stir and toil,
Ever their hearts burdened with cares,
No relief from fatigue do they enjoy,
They never know the taste of peace.

Sharp are their chins, and their lips strongly set,
Their muscles bear the message of life,
Figures of determination they look,
Their faces aglow as sunlight.

Ever do their large penetrating eyes
Brightly burn with yearnings acute,
No sooner is one craving satisfied
Than another springs up fierce.

Their spirits lose all zest and briskness
As their efforts achieve success,
Only then do they feel the freshness of youth
When there are chances of defeat.

The austere, the rugged, the difficult,
And all that which is not to be,
Are to them the sweetest inviting tasks
And whet their appetites the best.

Old jurisdictions they would relinquish
And win spheres of influence new;
Commodities stale but by even a day
Are apt to nauseate their souls.

Unrest is holy, worry is divine,
Failure is God's own element;
In paradise do they certainly live
Whose longings never reach an end.

THE CREED OF POVERTY

Unhoused exposed I live in my damp hut,
In through its roof the sun peeps and clouds pour;
Two boys, three girls, and man and wife, we here
Are huddled close as the cattle in farms.

The children run naked, myself half-clad,
The women, in rags, have but one full dress;
Hunger we check with coarse grains and leaves boiled,
Like swine we swallow food from earthen pots.

Two full meals on one day? That is a tale
Which we all remember the year throughout;
The winter we pass in beds of straw and hay,
And wallow in the mire during the rains.

To see a silver coin in others' hands
Is a matter of good luck in our lives;
And from the streets in fear our children see
How the inside of a school-building looks.

Poor I am, not Hindu or Christian,
Poverty is my description complete;
Poor I am, not above the beast-line yet,
I am a soul-less being, wheresoever born

INSPIRATION

Only once have I had a drink of strength,
And that draught has given birth to all my madness;
In one sip have I drawn the infinite soul,
And this has brought the universe under me.

In one moment was the door opened quietly,
Forthwith the heart was a fount of endless speech;
A random gust indeed touched me into bloom,
But on all sides the stream of fragrance rushed.

The gift came to me while I careless played,
Who knew then that it was a treasure priceless?
My manliness, energy, vital joy,
All these have been born of that unsought bliss.

Trifles make man; in the common lies the great;
In every moment's flesh and blood I am a god.

DEATH

Every moment I do my duty,
Every moment I taste my life and youth,
Such a moment animated with life
Should be the time for embracing my death.
No recollections from the past I nurse,
I count no dreams of a blissful future,
Of a life-in-the-present full of work
I want to make my death a common act.

When to die? Then, when life's fresh blood would
    flow
As vigorously as now that I live,—
Then, when the wish for self-assertion
From no signs of waning suffers eclipse,—
Then, when the power to enjoy the world
Would in plenitude maintain its course,—
Then, when the cogitation of weaklings
As to pros and cons divides not the soul.

Not like a dead animal I would die,—
Not like one whose heart hides no cosmic heat;
My last testament I would write at death
Myself, to declare the glories of the earth:
"It is energy that is life, its forms
Craving, lordship, love, warfare, defeat;
This ambrosia is not to be had
Except on this earth of mud, trees, and stones."

If God there be, and if it be His might
To satisfy man's prayers and demands,
And if death is bound to come,—I would pray
For a death full of madness, unrest, life.

THE MIND OF THE MASTER

Offsprings of cats and dogs are they, these slaves,
Or but moving instruments and machines;
Human beings' muscles and joints are not theirs,
Nor have they the blood that nourishes men.

I am not ashamed to undress myself
In the presence of groups of living tools,
One need be decent only to those that are men,
But the slaves were never as human known.

False and cowardly are slaves, mean traitors,
Immoral their women, households obscene;
Darlings of slaves? Eh? Their children and homes?
Their smiles and tears? Pooh! Of these herds of swine?

Literature and fine arts among slaves?
Did they ever enjoy humor and fun?
Are they not our servants by Nature made,
Hewers of wood and drawers of water?

Do slaves ever straighten the bones of their backs
To cast an upward glance into the skies?
Surely never can they offer response
To the things that make us frolic and sport.

Tame do they submit to the masters today,
All their fathers must therefore have been slaves;
Masters and slaves would differ on the globe
As long as the sun and the moon shed light.

THE MIND OF THE SLAVE

Do my masters ever walk on the ground
By moving their legs as I do mine own?
Do they through their nostrils exhale the breath,
The same that ever comes out of my lungs?

Men in the master's race are no doubt bold,
Dutiful, self-sacrificing, honest;
Their mothers and daughters and women-folk
Are the sisters of Alcestis, of course!

True love is known to the masters alone,
The masters alone know the art of play,
They alone know how to amuse oneself,
How can we dead creatures of all this know?

Do the masters ever shed tears of grief
Such as I do under bitter restraint?
Do they ever feel the pangs of despair
And sink exhausted into abysmal gloom?

Can my masters' souls be ever debased
By meanness, cowardice, and treachery?
Coarseness, ribaldry, license, lewd manners,—
Are these ever to be seen among them?

The flesh and blood of my masters' bodies
Methinks is made of some celestial stuff;
The begetting of children among their race
Is perhaps some super-human process!

Like Heaven's angels they look, my masters,
Not men and women of the earth are they;
Methinks there must be something extra
In all their pose, gesture, movement, speech.

THE GODS

The physician's aid I call for first,
Then to Mother Sheetala do I pray;
I bow down to Goddess Laksmee of course,
But first to farming and commerce I take.

My voice I train for songs, hands for the arts,
And fingers and toes to music and dance;
Long after, if at all, I care to know
How much has Benten given me of her skill.

They worship the Virgin Mother's image
And shout loud to Jesus and the scheduled saints;
But have they not kept their gunpowder dry
Before coming to services and hymns?

Do the Moslem man and wife build their life
On the votive offerings to the Pirs?
Do their laborers ever find the day's work
Accomplished through the verses of the Koran?

Boats, junks, ships, strong and varied in forms
Are first built by men to brave the sea-waves;
Then is invoked the mercy of the gods,
Kwan-yin, Neptune, Varoon, Water-Spirit.

It is the brain that makes man immortal,
It is by might that man becomes a god;
Why then has man prayed to the gods evermore?
Only because he is modest at heart.

Never have the gods been worshipped by man;
It is his own power that he adores;
Man is never the creation of God's,
God and the gods are the inventions of man.

THE UNIVERSAL TOUCHSTONE

It is the child that makes the parent famous,
The individual, the family;
It is again the citizen's greatness
That makes the nation known throughout the world.

Nobody cares to know your name or race,
Your clan no passport to your work is held;
By thermometers' and stethoscopes' aid
You would be sounded in every limb.

Your sweat they smell, they hear the pitch of your
voice,
Your legs' and arms' movements are counted sharp,
Your teeth are being tested against the stone,
They touch your saliva and taste your blood.

They apply the battery to your breast
To find the course of your nerval vigor;
And by the magnet they examine you
As to whose attraction governs your soul.

The testing laboratory is one,
The test is the same for all men on earth;
All individuals by this test
Set the life's standard for the human race.

THE POET'S MANIFESTO

It was but once that grief attacked my heart
And my eyes were flooded with streams of tears;
Yet their marks on the pages of the world
Would be read by generations of men.

Once did joyous smile blossom on my lips,
Yet on all lands has its lustre been cast;
Once did an adventure possess my soul,
Yet that fire would energize thousand minds.

Unrequited my love, I live forlorn,
That pang has purged the world's youths and maid-
ens;
Realized is my dream, my heart at rest,
A herald of peace I am for all times.

Why do you call my experience mine?
Is it not the life that everybody lives?
The eternal man's joys and sighs inspire
Even the humblest person's hopes and despairs.

I may have rebelled against creeds and codes,
But man am I of flesh and blood like you;
Therefore my songs would into crystals shape
Theories of life among diverse men.

THE HOME

One who has made me one's own is my home;
My home is one who rules ever my heart;
Brick walls or straw-thatch'd roofs do not make a
home;
The home is not great for its garden or court yard.

Down whose eyes'-eaves tears roll in my troubles,
Whose eyes in my happiness brightly beam
Even more self-forgetful than mine,
Whose breath energizes my life-blood's race,

Whose vital touch makes me enrich the world
With my personality's hundred gifts,
All whose steps, besides, are full of myself,
Whose god I am, whose friend, parent, guide I,—

That person, that heart is my happy nest;
The home is not mere stone, mortar, villa, cot.

One who the heart-walls of heaven-on-earth
Has cemented with the blood of human breast,
That angel, guard, brother, wife, husband, child
Lives in this world under the name of home.

SELF-EXPRESSION

Never do I think of serving mankind,
Yet surely a social servant I am;
Never do I speak of the fatherland,
Yet I am a genuine patriot.

My brain is pregnant with thoughts and fancies,
Great, mediocre, trivial, or wild;
Impossible it is to live in peace
While they teem imprisoned within the skull.

These I have lived up through fights, visions, sighs,
Poverty, smiles, despairs, dance, tears, what not;
Acquisitions they are through my own work,
Sickness, worry, sacrifice, enjoyment.

Of all these I would unburden myself,
Whatever be the medium I get;—
Laboratory, studio, paper,
Music chamber, writing table, clay or stone.

I can but express myself, my weakness,
My animality, my strength divine;
My forms would lead some to sink in despair,
But inspire others soldiers to become.

Only two functions my life has known:—
I can love and I can hate and thus be man;
This experience brings the human touch
To the eternal problems of the world.

You depend on energy, he on faith,
I believe in persons, in parties they;
You live in your own way, I live in mine,
Yet I learn from you, and the world from me.

HUMAN

I was born on this earth with limbs of flesh and
blood,
No greater faith I know than enjoying the world;
It is me that the world wants, and I want it too,
Without me the earth would like one blindfolded
roll.

Discipline, restraint, and self-control are but means
And instruments my energy to multiply;
It is their strength that makes a hero of myself
To lord it o'er the glories of this blissful world.

Shapes and forms of earthly things, and diverse
tastes,
Sounds that people the sky, and smells ensouling
the air,
And touch that imparts electric sparks,—all com-
bine
To animate my life and its career prolong.

Deathless I live as long as I quickened am;
Come ye, storm and stress, ever fresh and novel-
bred!
Let blood ebullient my body irrigate,
And the soul dance attendance on my senses all.

Millions of creeds and morals I would create
From my limitless exuberance when my life is full;
And the universe's beauteous self would move
To espouse me as her beloved god adored.

TO FIND YOUR RELIGION

The beats of your heart I would count
With my ears on your breast;
And I would feel your pulse to see
The dance-steps of your blood.

After fasts, I see, your appetite
Sets your blood on quick march;
And hearty meals energize it
All over your limbs.

Strong-muscled you are working hard
And evoking the blood's thirst;
Very well! But sound sleep would quench it
And raise its hopes afresh.

Have not the deaths of friends and parents
Brought forth floods from your eyes?
But has not your waterish blood
Been burnt red again by grief?

How oft have you laughed mouthful
And danced to heart's content!
Have not the crystals of joyous blood
Warmed then your lips and arms?

A home you have given the homeless,
Life to the dying people;
Has not their gratitude unlocked
The soft blood-gates of your heart?

Your religion, therefore, is
Whatever moves your blood;
Tears, smiles, work, play, eating, sleeping,
Gifts, prayers, love, and hatred.

THE CLIMACTERIC

No fire hadst thou within thy breast,
No words were on thy lips,
Thirst thine eyes did never have,
Nor hungry didst thou feel.

Madly did not thy hopes awake,
Not wild thy heart did dance,
Longings did not lead thee to tears,
Memories brought no smiles.

Wholly insensible lay thy limbs
Inert, irresponsive,
The petals of thy soul did sleep
Ever by night and day.

A revolution has set in in thy frame
As near thee I have come,
Right and left has each drop of thy blood
Moved to choose its own mate.

The chambers of thine inner self
Are now live with sweet dreams,
Overflooded now is thy soul
And inundates the world.

Thy beauty I have induced into bloom,
I have given thee thy youth's core;
The pole-star thou hast now obtained
To the magnet of thy life.

Deep determined thou walkest now
With charmed body and mind;
To move on earth by my impulse
Thou wert asleep thus long.

THE CRY OF THE POOR

Measure me not by the standard of man,
The poor are human beings only by voice;
A full man's limbs you see on me no doubt,
But they do not carry the fourth of a soul.

You move on earth alive, my life is death,
My wife and children make no home for me;
Your fancies create vast worlds in your minds,
Thereon you model your family and home.

My breast is dark, my heart devoid of fire,
Blindfolded my eyes, my ears stopped with wax,
To tempests my neck like weak trees I bend,
What makes you laugh and cry finds me like stones.

Mistake me not for man, then, though human-born,
Poor ignorant folks swell not mankind's force.

THE *PATRIE*

"It was in this land that I was born,
I wish, O Lord, I could die in this land!"
Is not this the burden of national hymns?
Could then any soul like the sky expand?

I am not responsible for my own birth,
I have no time to reflect about death,
I want to live in an immortal work,
Be it ever anywhere on this earth.

The land of one's birth no paradise is,
It is but the Chance-given inn for the being;
The true paradise is the field of your work,
That is the world whose creator you are.

Dost thou call thyself man? Surely then
Thou canst laugh and weep when thou touchest
man;
Thus enlarged thou, thy *patrie* is enlarged
By imbibing the life of all mankind.

Let energy always in volume grow
And always assume diverse novel forms,—
No other wish does Nature prompt;
Who would bury oneself in a single well?

My soul is not restless for here or there,
I feel strong if my mind is fixed somehow,
My home I make wherever I lay my heart,
And where else is the *patrie* but in the home?

THE ARTIST

Figures of clay or of bronze thou hast made,
Thou hast exhibited scenes on the stage;
The baby sees them from its mother's arms
And smiles and dances to senseless content.

Breezes of hopes thy lyrics have stirred up
In the adolescent's ripening mind,
The limbs of the youth thou hast inspired
With ambition's fire and love's superb might.

I know not what is the life thou livest,
Perchance differently keyed from my own;
Still in thy melodies have I found oft
The strains that I seek to keep me alive.

What is thy faith? What thy dogmas by birth?
Like poles asunder are we in views?
Yet the shapes and colors thou hast brought forth
Embody the soul that pushes me on.

Have I been irresponsive to thy call?
What then? Thousand others have heard thy voice;

Immortal thou, O creator, among men
If sincerely thou hast grieved and joyed.

Seeds numberless thou hast sown broadcast,
Could all be retained in a single spot?
I may have rejected some of thy gifts,
But others have gone mad to get the same.

Where is the person that does not create?
Which man or woman serves not social ends?
Each creator is a preacher to others,
All art is born a minister to life.

THE INDIVIDUAL

Be not anxious for the party or group,
Sects and societies are formed of themselves;
People care for individuals alone,—
Such as ever their self-assertion seek.

The band can be raised in a moment's time,
But hard to build up are the unit heads;
Such units in thousands does the world demand
As by their head and hands can draw all minds.

The life of Chaldaean Ur they must live,
They must suck dry Hellas and China's lore,
"Yamato damashii" they must absorb
And Eur-America's most recent finds.

Their own personalities they would display,
Not by their own friends would they sit to be
judged,
The world-standard would be their power's gauge,
Nursed on all earth they would serve their sects the
best.

Let such units rise to work even now
With creative determination high,
A new order would be evolved at once
Out of the present sects, parties, and states.

THE SONNET

I may be on my walk among the trees,
Or perhaps jostling a crowd of men;
Out of the movements of my swinging limbs
Emerges at once a sonnet into being.

Or while in the room my heart's pump is moved
By the lever worked from regions far off,
Sonnets in clusters have their birth forthwith
In the sweat of the brow and tears of eyes.

Or a vision I have while asleep,
Or perchance a memory haunts me on;
Groups of sonnets dissolved in vital blood
Quickly into crystals arrange themselves.

The sunshine and moonlight of a moment,
An instant's hopes and despairs deeply felt,
Every glance and every footstep,—
Are the dales where the sonnet-spirit lives.

But not a mere sum of moments is your life,
A geometric progression it is;
Sonnet to sonnet you may ever add,
Life would still be greater than all told.

I begin my laughter even while in tears,
A complex riddle within me I nurse;
This is why the soul cherishes epics
As Virgil, Kalidas, Dante, Milton wrote.

BREAK, BREAK, BREAK

The sun was broken to bring forth the earth,
And the broken earth soon begat the moon,
The hills were shot up by soil-breaking fire,
And streams have broken the barriers of hills.

Minerals decomposed form plant life,
Plants are pulverized to yield animal heat;
The past was dissolved to bring in the present,
Within the present the future struggles forth.

Every person is a plural being,
Duties and ideals break by moments,
Human life is revolution itself,
It does not understand a *status quo*.

Marks of breakings, crevices, erosions,
Architecture the world's self on all hands;
Never final, ever-failing is this earth
Whether of senseless or animate beings.

Where are Kapil and Aristotle now?
Even Kepler and Darwin are fading fast,
And radium's energy is bidding fair
To make the coal age a thing of the past.

What is progress but revolt and failure?
The real heroes are those that fail;
Endless existence belongs to that race
That is not deterred by the fear of defeat.

THE SOUL

For life I crave, I want life for ever,
I want to augment the power to live;
Through my own strength I would live a deathless
life,
And my salvation I would win by my might.

My demands and earnings, force and commands,
The rights and enjoyments that make my life,—
I mix them all with flesh and blood like beasts,
But never a beast all through I become.

My eyes are charmed by beauteous forms,
But formless beauty lives behind the eyes;
I am happy when I lord it over men,
But do I not then taste a bit of God's life?

My heat has warmed up the dispirited dead,
Awakened the cowards, and given them aims;
But beneath my heart's fire and might of arms
The unseen Phalgoo of ideals flows.

Ever through the senses' windows I peep out,
But do I not perceive through the super-sense-Me?
Right and wrong I base on profit and loss,
But does not duty ever prompt my heart?

Love lives in my animal limbs; the flesh
Draws flesh to sweeten and strengthen the life;
But limbless is love, it unfleshes human beings,
And to one-in-two adds the spirit of the world.

Unbodied, unmeasured, unknown something
Pervades my blood; would you call it the soul?
I know it as my fort, the cell of will
And power, wherefrom I govern all earth.

III

SIGHTS AND SOUNDS

ON THE HILL-TOP

So I climbed the hill and stood on its crown,—
There was the mid-day sun over my head;
Friendless I had traversed the mountain paths
But came into a home of high trees brave.

The roots of immortal pines formed thereon
The ribs of the breast of my hilly host;
The bright sun was pouring its juice of warmth
Through the openings of evergreen roofs.

Thin snowy clouds were floating brisk and fast
Across the deep blue body of the sky;
Far off, a solitary cloud-let sat
To enjoy the peace of a lonesome peak.

Single soul I swam in the sea of trees;
The forest spoke in the ocean's deep voice;
Diverse birds chirped a symphony chordless;
A rook's cry sawed the frozen silence of space.

My heart was swelling as I greeted was
With the soft kisses of the ozoned breeze,
And I was spurred by the tall pines that urged:
"Dare the skies, or die a lifeless death!"

Down below, the bluish bay bore its freight
Of little barges such as fishers use,
And I felt I had climbed a height indeed,
But, alas, the highest was yet to come!

ASSAOUAN ON THE NILE

A desert of golden sands on all sides
Washed by the burning sunshine from on high,
The thread of silver stream pulsates slow-paced,
Assaouan here guards the gates of Egypt.

Black peaks are peeping from the river-bed,
The unclouded sky sheds its blue downwards,
Date palms green the oasis on the banks,
Little sails on the barges whiten the scene.

Hill-environed regions of lifeless waste,
Between Libyan and Mokattam heights,
Mark off the wealth of Egyptian soils
From the arid rocks of Nubia's north.

Here are the quarries of the granite stone
That sculptors of the ancient pharaohs worked,
From here the boatmen carried their art-loads
Long down the Nile four or five hundred miles.

Here were carved the noble statues and sphinxes
For which Ammon's temple at Karnak is famed,
And the obelisk at Heliopolis
Where Plato studied the mysteries of life.

Makers of Amenheteps, both kings and gods!
Builders of pyramids and hill-cave tombs!
I see your half-done images on rocks,
Come and finish them, I would talk with you.

THE LINE OF PYRAMIDS

At Gizeh stands the imperial tomb,
The pyramid that Herodotus saw,
Herein lay the sarcophagus of stone
Bearing the mummy and jewels untold.

The builders of pyramids, were they men?
Could I have loved them if I had been then?
Could they call us their own if they appeared again?
In our modern songs would they find their strain?

Five thousand years ago they lived and died,
But like the mighty Tangs and the Caesars proud,
Patrons of letters and warriors bold,
Samoodragooptas and Charlemagnes all.

They knew to organize for twenty years
A hundred thousand masons for public works;
Not in an age this genius expired,
From dynasty to dynasty it flowed.

How did they live? Come to Sakkara old,
And see the serapeum of Ptah God's Bull,
Or the mastaba grave of Mera Lord,
Or at Der-el-bahree the terraced shrine.

Enter the chambers and see the paintings
Drawn in relief on walls, roofs, and pillars;
Energy personified their buildings are,
Simple grace lives in their colored work;

I see the hospitals for animals sick
And traders bringing Hindu goods from Punt,
The women are at their amorous dance,
Priests are sacrificing bulls to the gods.

Read the inscription at that grandee's feet:
"A virtuous husband, orphans' father,
An officer dutiful, just and strict;"
Shakespeare would have sung: "Here was a man!"

THE DELTA

Between Sahara and Arab sands
A freak of Nature is Lower Egypt,
Plenty of fertility's chosen land,
Oasised in an ocean of deserts.

Cloudless the skies are ever dry,
The Nile contributes its wealth of silt,
The cool Mediterranean cheers with breeze
The gardens and orchards of hundred hues.

Mulberries, there, hide merchants on camels,
Black soils of cotton, or yellow wheat, here;
And groves of bananas, sugar-canes, palms
Island the square gray huts of sun-baked mud.

A real Goshen is this deltaic plot,
The home of muscular strength, health, and joy;
Tall Moslem peasants "galabea"-clad
Are quick in response as their comrades call.

Far in the south the Abyssinian hills
Wrest the vapor from Indian monsoons,
Soils for Egypt are borne with the stream
That flows therefrom along a bed not wide.

This is the country of all mankind's morn,
Eternal link between the East and West,
The school that started the isles of Greece on;
Historic capitals were founded here:

Memphis, the oldest city of the world,
Near where Mohammed Ali's marble mosque stands,
And Alexander's port, with museums great
And the library that the Christians burnt.

MY NIGHT

If the night is dark and clouds rare
I look for comets in the sky;
Long, small, medium tails they display,
No matter what may be the month.

Only the nebulae I seek,
The well-formed stars I pursue not;
To the right and left my eyes turn
And fall at last on forces new.

Halley comes in seventy-six years
With grand disaster every time;
I am happy if I can find
Even those that commonplace are.

I see the small ones diverted
By attractions of masses big;
While afloat in the eastern skies
Perforce they are shunted aside.

But it is these lesser comets
That raise problems complex and hard;
One moment they live, but compel
Me to calculate night and day.

At times do meteors burn the air
And suddenly pierce the void;
Their flash survives not the first glance,
But of their comrades they foretell.

KOREA IN RAINS

It is pitch dark in Korea today,
The sky is pouring itself out in full,
As in Bengal the July rains deplete
The higher regions of their vapor wealth.

The mountain sides have been mantled over
By a panoply of clouds thin but as mists,
Million drops are bombarding them quick
Shot in succession as if through a sieve.

Hardly visible are the meadows at hand,
Still at their work are women in the fields,
Streams are running down the cottage eaves,
The waters gush swift through ditches and drains.

Water has swallowed the foot of the hills,
The cultivated plots are flooded deep;
Only as the train makes way through tunnels
Does the rule of rains in abeyance seem.

Rivers of lac or vermilion red
Seem on all sides in gutters to flow,
Or some animal arteries alive
Look dissected to exhibit the blood.

Or, currents of molten fire are they?
Stained red is the green vegetation, too;
Fair Korea with her rich fields of rice
Has a feast of crimson during the rains.

MOUNT TAI-SHAN

This is Tai-shan, the holiest
Of China's sacred mountains five,
With pines and "lotus flower peak,"
Where memories of ages dwell.

Here, as the "Shooking" story tells,
Emperor Shoon, of peasants born,
The model son and model king,
Offered sacrifice to Heaven.

Those were the days of patriarchs
And the rude beginnings of things,
Of faiths and songs that enshrined the hills,
Olympian and Vindhyan tops.

Long have its precipices borne
The footsteps of devoted men;
Paupers, princes, sages, poets
Have heard its falls and sung its scenes.

Confucius, the sage, who taught
The "Tao" of "superior men,"
Was here entranced as he beheld
The waves of peaks under the sky.

You see that spot, and read his words:
"Oh, how small is the world below!"
The spot and the words are holy yet
As Sinai and its Mosaic law.

Not the modest pilgrims alone,
It has drawn the ambitious, too;
To rival Shoon came Tsin Hwang-ti here,
From whom the land is "China" called.

Builder of the Great Wall, he bound
All the feudal states into one,
And with Napoleonic might
Rang out the old, enforced the new.

AT NANKING

The clouds have covered the sunshine of morn;
A grass-framed picture seems the old town-wall;
The swift Yang-tsze carries its life of blood;
And hillocks on both sides are capped in blue.

Junks with white sails pass up and down in rows;
Masts of boats have forested the canal;
A Delhî or Florence is here on view
With palaces, pagodas, parks, and tombs.

Queen of China's rice-zone and lotus-wealth,
Maker of poets, painters, craftsmen skilled,
Imperial city, the elders' pride,
Nucleus also of republic young!

IN NORTH CHINA

Muddier, yellower than the Yang-tsze,
The Hwang-ho pursues its destructive course
Like the turbulent Padmâ of Bengal;
And beyond, new vistas open all round.

Stalwart and warlike the people I see,
No more the sweet looks of the Southerners small,
Cotton soils and dry fields of wheat and corn
Accost me in the place of lakes and rice.

The peasants drive the plows with donkeys' aid,
Ill-clad they toil under the burning sun,
Cottages with walls and roofs made of mud
House big families of a dozen or more.

Here is the region of Cathay's dawn,—
Shantung, the land of Confucian fame,
Shensi and Honan with capitals old,
And Peking, the city that Kubla built.

AMONG ANIMALS

The woods draw me by their animal crowd,
Are not the animals quite human born?
Among their race I find myself at home,
In them I see the doubles of mankind.

Are you not crooked like the wily snake?
And like the tiger a ferocious beast?
How oft do we pick the quarrels of cats!
Are we not sometimes like the lion bold?

As peacocks are men to dancing attached,
As antelopes men are simple also;
Yet their lives are nets of spiders' intrigues,
We know how to give the mosquito's bite.

Changeful you are like the chameleon,
The toad's transformation also is yours;
Like the butterfly I am startled oft
If a shadow abruptly crosses my path.

The heat of the birds we nurse in our hearts,
This ever inspires our move to and fro;
Like the bees that always for honey thirst
We run from flower to flower for strength.

What is the explosion of human youth
But the bursting of the fly's larval form?
The chrysalis of life re-creates man
And endows him with voice and organs new.

The goats ever fight for females like men,
Rivalry in love bulls cannot endure,
Like men the nightingales sing to their loves,
And the cocks strike up love's excited dance.

The fishes give birth to offsprings untold
As men and women free from care of food,
In ants you find the hordes of nomadic tribes,
And settled cities in the hives of bees.

THE EARTH

Here on this earth my paradise I find,
I would not renounce it ever if I could,
Nor in search of novel worlds that might be
Would I care to let loose the reins of my mind.

The breast of the moon is splendid no doubt,
But her heart is no home of fire's warm glow,
Her nostrils bring no whispers of love's breath,
A burnt up mountain's figure is she.

She garments her nude self with the sun's gifts
As the raven in a peacock's plumage dressed;
A twin-sister she is to the earth although,
My soul could never find rest in the moon.

You speak of the Mars, that other planet
Where Lowell is founding a second earth?—
(God's rival, a Vishwâmitra he,
A Satan unpunished in this iron age!)

Capped with snow slabs are the poles of the Mars,
Only in spring they melt and water life,
Canals have brought a great green Egypt there,
Thanks to the skill of Martian sages.

But could they supply my human demands,
Plenty of the energizing caress of breeze?
Therefore with the sun's red fire in my breast
I choose to home in the arms of the earth.

JAPAN

Winter's glory is the chrysanthemum here,
The queen of Nippon in fragrance and tints;
The white cherry-blossoms furnish in spring
The hilarity of Yamato life.

The autumn gardens are brightened red
By the blood-hued leaves of dying maples;
And pine forests with their perennial green
Harbor the breeze that purges the lungs.

The seas embraced by hills put on their smiles
While the moon enlivens their skyey roofs,
Dancing rivulets born of singing springs
Afford constant music to listening ears.

Silk-smooth slabs of cedar like gold plates
Feed the eyes in cottages, inns, shrines,
And bright soft mats velvet the modest floors
With delicate peaceful feet to tread on.

The roofs of tiles and the paper walls
Look but parts of the landscape around;
Cleanliness is the religion of the homes;
As a limb of Nature does man here live.

MIDNIGHT BOATING

It is a midnight boating on the bay,
Moonless, windless, corpse-like rests the water;
The hills around look like the walls of a well
Or the folds of a lying black huge snake.

Or is the dark fortnight frozen into rocks?
The tent of the sky is raised on these posts;
Therein the hanging stars emit feeble light,
And the milky way from north to south.

I see the shores by the electric lamps,
As glow-worms in rows they brighten the huts;
With lines of fire they have striped the water,
And this makes visible the hills' somersault.

The Bears dance on the sea to the boat's beats,
And the shores send "geisha" songs and "samisen"
sounds.

A VILLAGE IN JAPAN

Hills on hills' shoulders, and hills on hillsides,—
Himâlayan verdure everywhere!
The sea of pines raises waves in the sky,
And casts on the gulf a shadow deep green.

Carpeted with velvet are the bright rice fields,
The grey mountain lanes meander up,
Tile-roofed cottages and straw-thatched huts
Dot the sea-coasts over with human life.

The yellowish green of thin young bamboo shoots,
And lotus stalks crowned with dawn-hued blossoms
Set off the kimono-clad women-folk
As on their backs their babies they carry.

Full-leaved tea-plants like rows of couchant sheep
Are hardly disturbed by travellers' talks;
But as the elders ply their fishing-rods
Urchins work havoc on cucumber-stands.

With drooping boughs supple willows not stout
Excite keen rivalry in the fair sex,
That would not yield the palm to senseless plants
In modesty of looks and light soft limbs.

AT MIYAJIMA

Where at the foot of sacred pine-clad hills
A Shinto shrine is lapped on by the sea,
There, at Miyâjimâ, the "isle of the shrine,"
Between Nippon and Shikoff I spend my days.

Here the tidal waters wash the base
Of the "torii" gate mahogany-made,
And on briny sands left dry at ebb-time
The lovely antelopes gambol and frisk.

Maples are acquiring autumnal red,—
The burnt gold of Bengal's mango in spring;
Hard by, the pines are gorgeous in fresh green,
Afar, they shed the glorious sky-blue.

Like paintings drawn on hillsides are the inns,
Abodes of peace in maple and pine groves;
Only one voice here keeps silence alive,—
The songs of joyous springs beneath the floor.

AN EVENING

The grey clouds have acquired a yellow tinge
Where the sun impinges its farewell rays,
Other patches of jet-black clouds hard by
Through hidden fire seem besmeared with blood.

Bluish lava of frozen cloud-layers
Has framed, as it were, the entire sky;
The eastern horizon and the mountains there
Are with gloomy hues accoutred and capped.

The sun is knocked up by its day's hard toil,
The tired world also wants respite from work,
Exhausted the hills look reclining flat,
The thatched cots' eyes seem arrested by sleep.

The whole earth has put on its sable robes,
Lamps have not been dressed in the hamlets yet,
A dreamy land of spirits and elves
Appears to have lent its vagueness to man.

SUNSET IN CALIFORNIA

This the westernmost city of the world,
Sanfrancisco-*cum*-Berkeley this;
Here into the Pacific's deep blue waters
The dying sun takes daily plunge.

Here is concentrated the grandeur greatest
Of sunset that the earth can show;
Blood-stained shine the skies, the ocean, too,
Even the wide breast of the land.

North and south is the western sky ablaze,
O'er lanes and lawns china rose seems to bloom,
Mirror-like polished streets burn in warm red,
Panes reflect the parting day's glow.

Ruddy are the sand-dunes tinged on sea coasts
Against which waves numberless dash;
Over green tree-tops on bare barren hills
Play ripples of orange red.

Ranches and farms on fields of vermilion
Plowmen seem to furrow with spades;
And on the orchards of apples and pears
The clouds their crimson glory shed.

An uncommon light on the gorgeous west,
Is ever Nature's wealth at eve;
Of that the highest effulgence enshrouds
This westernmost edge of the western world.

CROSSING THE ROCKIES

Mount Kânchan-janghâ's glassy waves
Just to my right and left at dawn;
Methinks I am gliding swiftly through
An ocean of snow dusts white.

The Rockies' back seven thousand feet
In Utah state was but simple height;
Tennessee Pass ten thousand high
In Colorado I scale this morn.

Drowsy snows gave an eerie light
Reflecting the full moon's pallid smile;
But the snows set in the sky's blue frame
Are burning bright in warm sunshine.

Wealth of verdure Himâlayan
Rarely carpets the Rockies' sides;
Few stunted firs and lonesome pines
Furnish apology for trees.

Monster-like vast granite boulders
Mount guard, erect or couchant flat;
And through the lanes of weird stone blocks
Half-frozen waters' rivulets dance.

Fountains murmur music to ears,
Ice floats along with the currents;
Here and there slabs of compressed snow
Hide from sight the stream's onward flow.

Reddish hills wall up both the sides
Of a narrow treeless defile,—
Partly the scenes these of the Western Ghats
While one descends into the Kankan coasts.

BLEAK DECEMBER

It is December; trees have shed their leaves;
The grains have been sheaved by farmers away;
Miles and miles I see gilded orange bright
By withered shrubs, grass, and long stalks of maize.

Snow dusts are flying madly through the streets,
Nostrils and eyes weep, the ears are bitten numb;
Death has gripped the avenues of town elms;
The meadows not far look like forests burnt brown.

Solid frozen is the Iowa's current,
A meandering thread of whitish snow,—
In disguise a blessing, it affords good time
To youths and their girls in their love's skating
dance.

Showers upon showers of powdered snow
Have noiselessly covered the roofs and yards,
The roads are buried even three feet thick,—
A desert of dry milk froth all white.

Houses in cities have the heat from steam,
Farms in the villages are almost dead,
Nature is arrested wholesale by cold,
Creation's fire has been banished from earth.

Only perhaps in view of the coming feasts
On merry Christmas and New Year Eves
Women are making cakes in rural homes,
And the tongues of children water thereto.

SPRING

Again has fresh life burst on the old earth,
Nature is shivering through a vital urge,
The incubus of snows is off the fields,
Molten spirit courses free in the Charles.

No more do dusky fogs blind the eyes,
Villas on Boston hills seem quite at hand;
Doors wide open, the world enters the room,
Every live being is out tasting the earth.

Resurrection is on amongst dead trees,
Living leaves are shooting out inch by inch,
The squirrel to bask in the sunshine warm
Layeth her head on the breast of the branch.

Verdure is manifest at spots on lawns,
Pigeons fly into men's arms in the parks,
With changed garments around man keeps pace,
The senses are stirred by the new year's youth.

SPRING IN AMERICA

Not in America does the spring bring forth
The honeyed leaves of Indian mango trees,
No "palâsh" here stands with enormous boughs
To display fire-buds in the upper air.

The "bokool" blossoms' fragrance is not borne
Into the rooms by the blast of the breeze,
Bees in millions are not busy here
To suck at the flowers' lips their juicy souls.

Fresh green foliage has overspread the skies,
The fields are furnishing their floral feasts,—
Some painter in his color-studies absorbed
May have dipped his brush in the wealth of life!

Cotton flakes white seem to have enveloped
The short-statured pears with flowery vests;
Like guinea-gold are the young leaves on twigs
Of other trees that brighten the garden groves.

Red and white are the tulips swollen proud
Like the "champa" that blossoms low at your feet,
The tiny forsythias yellow the fence
Before they make way for the sprouting leaves.

Sparrows are coming from the bush to the roofs,
Meadows are astir with the ducks' loud quacks,
In stately style do the swans move their necks
While they enjoy their royal swim on streams.

AFTER A SPRING SHOWER

Spring showers have refreshed the foliage life,
All earth is now satined with the greenest grass,
The crystal stream is lapping against the banks,
The warm air is drunk with the smell of damp soils.

With boys and girls are the mothers at play
Under the pear trees young in half-formed leaves,
Couples of sweet-hearts are happy ensconced
In the smug nooks of forsythia bush.

Yellow dandelions have starred the fields,
Plentiful as "ganda," the winter's gift;
In clusters hang white lilacs from the shrubs,—
Images of budding love's soft tender soul.

Walls are hidden under creeping ivy leaves,
Wistarias speak through violet lips,
The caws of crows mix with the buzz of flies,
Multi-colored life reigns in streets and groves.

THE BLUE HILL

Drenched in the rain I am out on the Blue Hill,
Gray Jersey cows are grazing in the farms,
The forsythias are being shorn of blooms,—
And their bright yellow by green leaves replaced.

Large cups seduce me from their garden homes,
Seated on the crowns of vigorous green stalks,—
Tulips youthful, six-petalled blossoms they,
Grand in colour, white, yellow, lotus-red.

Narcissuses, peers of "tagar" white,
Display at the core their yellow cups red-fringed,—
Pure marble plates, six-rayed stars on thin stems,
Boldly to the air their bosoms they unveil.

Carnations ruddy white arrest my eyes,
Green-perianthed, and with corollas thick;
Golden leaves are darkening into green on trees,
Apple flowers on the grass I mistake for hail.

STATUE OF LIBERTY

Thou, through whom alone man differs from beast,
Whose absence dehumanizes mankind,
Who leadest man take the Creator's stand,
Who inducest schemes and thoughts scale the skies,

Whose eyes guide aptitudes attain full growth,
Who aidest free movements through heaven and
earth,
Who inspirest man the impossible to do,
Who buildest a world of unending hopes,

Whose essence is ever new, fresh, mobile,
And admits of adjustments by days,
Who enrichest man's life with nature's gifts,
Simplicity, straightforwardness, ease,

Through whom is achieved the completest being
Of the child, man, woman, society, race,
With whose extinction is driven underground
The self-hood of all persons and nations,

Whose message is the basis of character,
Origin of morals, and source of creeds,
Energy behind all world-forces, Thou,
O Liberty, the very fount of life!

SHAKTI (ENERGY)

In ripe corn's golden silk her I have found;
On the sky's broad breast does she reveal herself;
Numberless messages through air she sends
Which the clouds on their wings convey to me;
Without effort she has her soul announced
In the blooming flowers' fragrance and tints.

In the noisy hubbub of thronging crowds
Have I heard her voice musical and clear;
Her balmy breath through nostrils I have drunk
While lonesome on the silent peaks of hills.

With loving hands has she caressed my limbs
Applying the soft beams of cool moonlight;
And on the bright waters of the ocean
The speeches of her eyes I have perused.

In the sun-burnt regions of deserts wild
Her alone I have companion found;
Through the million drops of rain from on high
Her presents of pearl-beads have come to me.

How often silvery pure has she smiled
Over the tree-tops glistening with snows!
And in the murmuring songs of brooks
Her spirit's current has come flowing down.

In all my tears and smiles and hopes and fears
A personality through her I claim;
In darkness, however, I find her best
When quite alone in the midnight dead.

IV

"WHAT LOVE MIGHT BE, HATH BEEN, AND IS"

IN THE STATE OF NATURE

(From "The Beginnings of the Swiss Republic")

To lay the foundations of the temple of life
They felt no need for auspicious flowers.

No hymns of priests did their souls make one,
They found a free spot between earth and sky;
No lawns and halls were crowded with guests
While the cementing of their hearts was on.

The rolling waters made music thereto,
The pipe was played by the sonorous wind,
Stars in clusters were witnesses above,
And the fire of two loving hearts below.

THE WOMAN'S FANCY

Full of grace is his body's build,
Large-souled heroic youth is he;
Attracted by my little heart's strength
Down from heaven he has been brought.

The silent smile of my calm eyes
His life's sole enthusiasm is;
He likes to win fame by his work
Because that would add to my pride.

Throughout the land his name is carried
On account of his daily deeds;
His greatness I do not understand,—
In warfare, in arts, or in science?

For the good of the people or the state
Perchance he has duties stern;
If into fire he has to run
My face still shines before his eyes.

While far from me he lives alone
In my memories home he makes;
Even in lonesome silent forests
My voice he can distinctly hear.

By my side his is a baby's heart,—
As it were, a child or brother mine;
Love's whole self he is and finds in me
His darling, sister, mother, all.

The whole universe we fill out,
Though but two souls, myself and he; .
He is the ruler of the world,
And me? I live only by loving.

MAZZINI'S THOUGHTS REGARDING MAGDALENE

(From "The Youth of Mazzini")

Unseen sweetness is she in my dutiful life,
As formless fragrance mingles in the tempest's being;
Through all my emotions and heavings runs her breath;
Hues to my activity she gives like sunlight;
Hers the hand that pumps the blood of my heart;
Hers the life-breath moving through the forge of my lungs.

Energy fierce, efforts vast, move determined
To one end relentless, dreadfully serious,
Stern responsibility, cataclysmal might,—
All these are my companions ever on earth;
Even in such a forest has the jasmine blossomed forth,
Even with Vesuvian eruptions it sends perfumes.

Her soul's tenderness makes me impart grace to strength,
Under her eyes life's value has risen hundredfold;
Fresh glories and meanings I see everywhere now,—
It is her wealth added new to my own austere eyes.

THE *VITA NUOVA* EXPLAINED BY DANTE

(From "Dream-Beatrice")

I love her limbs' build beautiful and strong,
Soft round arms, smooth neck, face bright with
health's bloom,
Marble-pure skin-pride, dawn's smile on lips,
The cool stream of love's light in tender eyes,

The youthful bosom, flowing silken hair,
The glossy pools of eyes beneath brows still,
Gentle voice, messenger from heart's recess,
Balmy breath's current, proof of spotless life,

Steady graceful gait, head erect, kindly gaze,
Sitting and standing simple, body straight.

But most of all I love her soul unseen
Charmed and concentrated by the spell of love,—
Of which the brows, eyes, lips, face, movements
Are but external expressions and forms,—

Whose real utterance is heart-beats quick,
Sweet tears from eyes, and sensitizing touch,—
The speechless urge from which is a holy call
For my limbs and mind in devotion to pause.

SHAKOONTALA'S TEARS REMEMBERED BY DOOSYANTA

(From "The Expiation of Doosyanta")

"Speak once, O darling mine, that thou wouldst not
Forget me ever in thy mind;
I would manage to live in my limbs
Solely on the strength of that word.

"To thee my life I have surrendered for good,
In thy hands would it ever rest;
If once a heart be given away in full
Can it be afterwards taken back?

"Million times a day only one word
Would ring on the strings of my heart:
'Beside myself have I nothing mine own
That I can, dear, present thee with.'

"What I have once given away to thee, sweet,
Oft would I give thee, O soul of my soul,—
A little heart, the gift of a simple girl,
But full and rich with thoughts of thee.

"Thy shadow I am, master of my being,
This is my one happiness on earth;
My hopes, dreams, and memories, all would tell
Ever and oft: 'Myself is thine.'

"My home thou art, wheresoever livest thou
Far from this hermitage of saints;
Thy image would on the plate of my soul
Remain engraved ever bright."

The maiden's eyes burst into a flood of tears
As these words her inner self opened out;
That picture of bitter pang I had drawn
With a piercing steel on my heart.

WHILE HE IS AWAY

No more to her hair she attends,
Nor cares she for ornaments now;
Two wells of peace are her deep eyes
In reflective satiety fixed.

Fast closed her lips are always now;
Her face with paleness' glory shines,—
Beneath the shroud of a double cloud
Like the moon that is fading wan.

A single word comes out with her breath
Whether asleep or awake,
All the channels within her breast
With the stream of that word are filled.

For food appetite she has lost,
And is not refreshed in sleep,
Speechless she does her household work
All lonesome; in that is her rest.

Where darkness lies concentrated deep
And where people no bustle make,
There her heart by day and by night
In soft slow beatings palpitates.

How often she wakes while at bed
Startled, quivering, and sheds tears!
For one soul in her eye-drops flow
Million prayers of her heart.

The deathless tie of souls she adores,
She minds not beauty, wealth and fame;
A piece of heaven is the deepened life
Of a woman in the longings of love.

FAUST RELATING THE GRETCHEN EPISODE TO MEPHISTOPHELES

(From "Faust's Experience")

No weakness is love, it is strength infinite;
In the bonds of senses two souls get free.

Subjection is reckoned priceless glory
In only one sphere of human life's run,—
The sacred slavery of love is that,
Man and woman's mutual dependence.

Unrestricted freedom each surrenders,
Each abandons the ways of one's sweet will;
Sanctified the union of love becomes
By the equal sacrifice of each.

Though unbodied itself, the foundations of love
Lie in the earthly mud of flesh and blood;
Without senses surely no love could be born,
The senses are the golden gates of heaven.

Tears, sighs deep, heartbeats loud, and halting
    speech,
Eyes' thirst, hopes of lips, and hunger of arms,
Trembling limbs, senseless self, and blood's race
    fast,—
Each pours into life a moment's health and vigour.

In such a moment is tasted endless life,
Man and woman do the impossible through love.

THE LOVER'S WOMAN

(From "Browning and Barrett")

Never of earth's flesh and blood are woman's limbs
formed,
Kindliness and love in human being's shape is she;
In her eyes dwells mercy, endless good in her touch,
She breathes self-sacrifice, and speaks freedom and
trust.

Her heart is the home of an ocean profound
That is brimful of self-denying sympathy's milk;—
A series of offerings is woman's whole life,
Disinterested devotion's stream is her blood.

A fountain of never-failing energy is she;
The petals of heart she silently opens out
By the gentle rays from her loving tender eyes;
And spirit super-sensual her arms' embrace gives

Only one religion abides in the woman's soul,—
She makes man of animal, and god of mankind;
Teacher of restraint and sense of duty is she;
By her is filled with courage even the coward's heart.

And if contact with her body's muscles and limbs
Leads a human being immortal to feel,
Is not woman the very goddess of the world?
And are not the organs of sense God's tabernacles?

AN EPISTLE OF MAZZINI

(From "The Youth of Mazzini")

How many gifts have I received from her
Fragrant with the smell of her heart!—
A leaflet, a flower, a lace,
That decked the tresses of her hair,

The ribbon of warm-red silk that was tied
To the dress of her heaving breast,
A lock of golden hair that wantonly danced
Down her sides and neck and back,

A handkerchief with her own fingers sewed
Under eyes steadfast and intent,
Every stitch in which is her love-talk
With the dearest star of her being,

A volume whose pages she has perused
And marked with pencil for me,
In marking which her sensitive fingers
Shivered glad in the very act,

Numberless letters all with writing filled
In her pearl-like characters small,
Whose every line is the mouthpiece true
Of genuine tears, smiles and joys.

How oft with the fire of her breast
Before despatching she warms her gifts!
Them she makes the messengers of her soul
With hot stamps of thousand kisses.

But every moment her life she sends
Along with the breeze of her breath;
Her spirit I receive in the day's sunshine,
Her eyes in the moon and stars at night.

REPENTANT DOOSYANTA REFLECTING ON WOMAN

(From "The Expiation of Doosyanta")

The genius of woman lies in love,
Therein her human mission she fulfils.

It is woman who loves and in love does live,
Man knoweth not what is that thing called love;
In man's life love is one of thousand acts,
Love is the only substance in woman's heart.

Self-effacing atoms her elements are,
Cares for others form powder for her limbs,
Thoughts for others make her consciousness' stream,
Ever through her veins flow prayers for others.

Her self-surrender endows all senses
And their delights with transcendent re-birth;
Her soul charmed in the magic bonds of love
Delivers a soul from imprisoned self.

Temple of renunciation is her frame,
Muddy, material, mortal although;
The love that oozes in the female heart
Is the fount of discipline among men.

Never a half of man's being is woman,
Womanhood is a complete distinct force;
The heavenly self-sacrifice of hers
Brings glory to all that is done by man.

V

PERSONALITY

ROBERT BROWNING

Approach not Robert Browning ye who want
Success, tranquillity, or peace of life;
Solution of conflicts, and harmony
Do not furnish themes of his plays, songs, and tales.

A deep plunge he took into vital sap
To perceive, explain, convey life's own being;
Life is but movement, unrest, revolution,—
A story of fight and grand defeat.
Man is not he who is content with success,
He is man indeed who ever failure seeks;
Daily to seize fresh future is his one care,
To grasp the moon, up into the skies to fly.

Hair-splitting critic is Browning; he paints
Eternal soul and finite body's strife;
Heroes, hermits, lovers, priests, scholars,—all
Bear on flesh and blood endless yearning's marks.
Wildly in the breast of men and women
Surges the same Paracelsian word:
"Immense am I, immortal is myself,
Grow I would, break I would, though bound in
mud."
Life is not in any moment exhausted,
In any nucleus, person, or race;
To fail is the nature progressive man's,
New hopes live on through despair, doubt, death.

Teacher of efforts, of fruition careless ,
O thou world's greatest, best critic of life!
Thine is the modern Geetâ's gospel of hope
And work for its own sake, O seer, energist bold!

WALT WHITMAN

No human being indeed is Walt Whitman,
Yankeestan's Niagara Falls is he;
Impetuosity of cataracts
And tumult cataclysmal fill his being.

Language's fetters sundered he has,
He has violated the rhythm so-called;
Delight he finds in smashing to pieces
Formulae and tastes which the market rule.

Broken had been the shell of Egypt and Greece
For bringing into life an Europe young,
Spurning Europe defiantly arose
The Americans' home in lands new found;

In this America, again, was the East
Transformed to pioneer the Middle and the West;
Further revolution was brought on earth
By steam propelling carriages and boats;

Revolution in revolution's wake,
Changes upon changes, freshness refreshed,—
All this is monumented in the song
Of the Yankee people, called "Leaves of Grass."

Leaves of grass? Yes, it was in grass that Whitman
The vital impulse of the universe found,—
In man's daily stirs, frets, sleep, sports, sex-life
The liberation of his endless soul.

What increaseth life, energy, and joy,
And resists the onset of grief and death,—
Is men and women's universal creed;
Superfluous all other dogmas preached.

ASOKA

Was Asoka but an ascetic king,
That grand monarch of a united Ind?
Let us see: was it not he that followed close
Kautilya's Machiavellian code?

Did the "Artha-shâstra's" teachings inspire
Self-mortification in princely flesh?
Had he not drunk of Shookrâchârya's lore
That finds in politics the highest art?

To Central Asia his men he sent,
Bearers of his own and empire's names;
Syria, Greece, Macedon, Epirus,
Egypt and Kyrene also heard the same.

The world's gifts he brought into his own land,
At Pâtalipootra the Hindus learnt Greek;
Medical doctors he despatched far West
And his ambassadors to the great powers.

As sovereign universal he summoned
All rulers to Dhamma's supreme control;
What was that Dhamma? Not a creed of retreat
From the world, but India's message of life.

Let us see: was it not he that inscribed
His commands on rocks all ages to guide?
Surely he enjoyed the majestic sway
And domestic bliss as earthly king!

If such the self-less renunciation be
Of which hermits' spiritual souls are made,
Were not the Caesers and Fredericks quietists
then,
Tang Tai-tsung, Napoleon, and Peter?

VIRGIL

No mere antiquarian thou,
Latin hero, Virgil!
To old tales thou hast given shape
At thy own fancy sweet.

The blaze of mid-day sun thou hast poured
Upon national life's dawn;—
Forefathers are surely supermen
If offsprings have success!

Civil wars had ceased, and conflicts
Of republican mobs;
Powerful Augustus was enthroned
In Roman empire new;—

The queen of all lands then became
The land of the Latin race,
Hence, in thine eyes, as in Livy's,
Heaven indeed was Rome.

Wherever success would crown
The efforts a people makes,
An "Aeneid" it would write to prove
Golden childhood's promise.

As the gods wished, Aeneas had left Troy
To seek Latian shores,
Through his exploits thou hast foretold
A "Bhavisya Puran."

Homer's disciple, inspirer
Of Dante's and Mazzini's,
Teacher of patriotism thou
Of all ages and climes!

DANTE

By Beatrice's love, O Dante, stirred,
Thou, prince of Florence's poets!
In the love of woman thou foundst
The nucleus of the infinite world.

Cavalier bold, city-father stern,
Death-sentenced, exiled, thy life was
The full mine of experiences rich
That the Middle Ages could give.

No language-wealth, no unity's strength,
No empire's glory in thy time
The Italian enjoyed; hence thy voice
To people's ears raised trumpet-call.

A new vitality acquiredest thou
When but nine years thou wert of age,
The innocent looks of a simple child
Smiled with eternal blessings on thy soul.

The gift of a moment from the female heart
Brought immortality to thy aims,—
Revived the "Aeneid" of Virgil, thy guide,
Inspired Mazzini freedom to preach;

Thence came also Purgatory's cleansing,
Hopes, and ideals for mankind;
Woman's eyes then are not made of trifling flesh,
Heaven speaks through her love-charmed glance.

NAPOLEON

No avatar of brute force wert thou,
Child of Corsica, and servant of France!
Napoleon, thou wert parented by
Superb Imagination herself.

Thy soul wanted to give noble shapes
To ideas vast and wide as the skies,
The exploits of the French gave thee but scope
To display thy creative genius' strength.

To save the *patrie* from foreign tyrants
The infant republic sought thy hands' aid;
Signalled by thy self-confident fingers,
The volunteers achieved easy success.

Democracy's guard! No aggressor thou,
The aggressors lay humbled at thy feet;
Fortune made thee *dominus omnium*
Over astonished Europe awhile.

Protector of industries, science, arts,
Source of mass-education, legal codes,
Apostle of empire's renown as well,
Thou art the idol still in all French hearts.

Not France alone thy debtor thus, thy work
Has ushered in the modern age's lights;
German unity's father thou, herald
Of national movements, and Italy free.

GOETHE

Strange was thy life from beginning to end,
Goethe, thou greatest among Germans born!
It was a melting-pot, a crucible grand
That boiled what conflict most into a mass.

Sweet fancy's companion thou at soul,
Yet Weimar state was piloted by thee;
Ever on poesy's ocean afloat,
Yet in science's exact methods skilled.

Students today of positive knowledge
Recognize in thee a monument great,—
Through thee the flower is but leaf transformed,
And the brain continues the spinal cord.

How elastic could thy heart ever be
To bear a new woman's love every day!
How didst thou manage to be set aflame
Each time with equal passion sincere?

Werter, Wilhelm, Hermann, and Faust have come
Of that experience sea-like complex,
Into the frame of thy own full-lived life
Thou hast grouped the problems of whole mankind.

Schiller, whom the stormers and stressers adored,
Was thy most personal intimate friend,
Yet never didst thou lose thy calm Greek poise
In the abandon of his romantic dreams.

Thy country groaned under Napoleon's heels,
Yet thou his glad associate couldst be!
Thou didst not join in movements national,
But thou art the fountain of German *Kultur!*

DWI-JENDRA-LAL ROY

With dreams and memories hast thou destroyed
The bounds of the spiritless real world;
Crystals of energy hast thou strained off
From the solution of Young Bengal's life.

In medieval ages Hindustan had
Springs of activity and prowess,
These thy dramas have let loose and free
To irrigate a dead Saharan soil.

Nebulous had been the ideals long,
Formless wandered the people's visions,
Undefined the objects of love and pride,
Not clearly known what to fear and hate;—

Then camest thou to furnish the goal of life
And exemplars embodying duty's call,
The alien hast thou marked off from one's own,
With jealousy hast thou enriched the soul.

Victory or defeat thou countest not,
Thou but watchest the race of human blood,
With equal earnestness dost thou smell
Life's odor,—in advance as in downfall.

In heaven there flows discontent, conflict,
Animation, enthusiasm, passion;
That current is continued below
As thy idealism and longing high.

Schiller of the twentieth century
  Thou, India's Dwi-jendra-lal Roy!
Inebriated thou wert with the light
That nobody sees on the breast of the earth.